Talking to the Wild

TALKING

to the WILD

THE BEDTIME STORIES

WE NEVER KNEW

WE NEEDED

Becky Hemsley

TALKING TO THE WILD AT WILDMARK PUBLISHING

COVER DESIGN BY LERAYNNE

leraynne.myportfolio.com

EMAIL INQUIRIES: info@talkingtothewild.com

ISBN 978-1-7398245-1-8

For John, Rory
and Archie

Thank you for
inspiring me
everyday xx

Hi, come in. Sit down. Make yourself comfortable. And if you're reading or listening to this in bed, snuggle in and make yourself even more comfortable.

Maybe you're reading or listening to this on your commute or on the way to visit family or friends. Maybe you're walking on the beach or through the woods or in the snow. Or maybe you're sitting by a pool on holiday somewhere nice and warm.

Wherever, and however you are reading this, the message is the same; this story is about you.

I say story but it's actually a collection of poems; bedtime stories that we were likely never told as children but that can bring us comfort, peace, healing, joy and gentle reminders as we grow. And, because these are poems that I've just arranged in some semi-logical order, you don't need to read from start to finish. You can dip in and out as you need. Some days you'll need comfort. Some days you'll want joy. And some days you'll just need to feel heard. Validated. Seen.

And I hope that's what this book gives you. I hope you get lost in the words and find yourself.

Enjoy

Becky xxx

Important Stuff

- This is still your story even if you are not 'she',
  'he', 'you' or 'they' as is written in each poem.

- Some of these poems may trigger difficult and painful
  emotions or memories. At the end of the book, you can
  find contact details of places you can reach
  out to for support. Please don't struggle alone.

- I am from middle England and I write my poetry with my own accent in
  mind which means the poems rhyme or near-rhyme for me. I hope that,
  even if some poems don't rhyme for you, you can still hear the messages
  behind the words.

- I've often been asked who my favourite poets are, and I have to admit
  that I am just inspired by beautiful words – whoever it is that wrote them
  or spoke them. Words have the power to transcend time and space and
  can make people and places live forever. They can make us feel things
  we didn't even realise we were feeling. They can build – and tarnish –
  reputations. They can connect us to others and to ourselves. Edward
  Bulwer-Lytton once wrote that "the pen is mightier than the sword" –
  and I think he might have been right.

and now for poetry...

Contents

Part One

The World

they'll try and tell you

there are seven

wonders of the world

when in fact

there are millions

magic

you tell me that I'm childish
seeing magic in the world
that there's no room for enchantment
on this scientific earth

you give me explanations
and you hand me charts and graphs
for you say there can't be magic
in the company of fact

but I'll argue that there's magic
in a new-born baby's cry
and in how that baby heard
it's mother's heart beat from inside

I'll tell you that it's magic
how a butterfly exists
that there's something most spellbinding
about metamorphosis

there's magic in the differences
between each flake of snow
and in people finding footprints
from a million years ago

I'll tell you that it's magic
how the tides move with the moon
and how the sun can split a raindrop
into seven different hues

it's magic how a spider
weaves a complex fragile web
and how all the words of years of songs
are stored inside our heads

but you'll tell me there's no magic
for this all can be explained
yet, to me, there's magic dancing
in the workings of our brains

see the danger is our knowledge
means there's little awe to spare
but if we stop looking for magic
then we'll never see it there

live to live

not to die

the human race

we're part of one big race
and that's exactly what we do
we race from place to place
because we've so much we must do

but does it all need doing
or do we run the race because
everybody else is running
and we're trying to keep up?

we're racing ever forward
barely stopping to look back
rarely standing in the moment
to give thanks for what we have

instead we're always chasing
'til the winner's crowned 'the best'
for we seem to think to win at life
we have to beat the rest

yet the glory's not in winning,
it's in how we take our time
it is more about the race itself
and less the finish line

see what we must remember
most of all about this race
is that it doesn't pay to come in first
but rather in last place

and yet we keep forgetting,
and it's such a dying shame,
for no matter how we run our race
the finish line's the same

we are, all of us,

pieces of one

big puzzle

a perfect fit

I take his hand in my hand
and our fingers knit together
in a way we give no thought to
like it's been this way forever

see it doesn't seem to matter
whether family, friend or lover
it's just amazing how we humans
are designed to hold each other

my hip supports the little one
who sits there on my left
for it's there she hears my heartbeat
and it calms her through my chest

they hug me and I hug them back
and gently rest my head
in the warm and waiting me-shaped nook
that's carved against their neck

he leads me to the dancefloor
as the music starts to play
and my hand sits on his shoulder
whilst his arm's around my waist

each part is like a jigsaw piece
each hand and neck and hip
and they're waiting on the moments
where they're destined just to fit

we all experience

the same things

differently

the wind

the sapling and the oak tree
stood together side-by-side
the sapling small and fragile
and the oak tree tall and wide

they turned their leaves to sunlight
and they welcomed steady rain
for their common goal to grow
meant that their needs were quite the same

but at dusk one day in springtime
a strong wind came from the west
and it blew 'til almost midnight
when it tired and it left

to the oak it had been gentle
it had danced about his roots
it had whispered to his branches
like a friend just passing through

but to the little sapling
it had screamed in disarray
it had clawed at him relentlessly
and snatched his leaves away

and the oak tree asked next morning
why the sapling looked so sad
when the wind had only blown one night
and hadn't been that bad

and the sapling looked disheartened
at the oak so wide and tall
"but you only lost one leaf," he said
"whilst I have lost them all"

our differences

are our magic

starlight

he carries specks of starlight
in a little silver pot
and they tell him that he's strange
because he has something they've not

see they've already decided
that he isn't worth a lot
yet if only they looked closer
they'd find magic in his pot

they never think to ask him
what it is he keeps within
for they'd rather speak in whispers
that he doesn't quite fit in

see they think that being different
is a lonely, scary shame,
they don't realise that our magic
lies in how we're not the same

yet when it's dark they search for
all the light his starlight casts
but they don't know it's his doing
'cos they never cared to ask

and even if they asked him
they'd be likely to misjudge
and instead of silver starlight
they'd see only specks of dust

roll up

roll up!

the greatest show on earth

welcome to our circus
it pulls in quite the crowd
for it charges no admission
and says all welcomed and allowed

we hope that you'll enjoy it here
but one thing if I may
once here we'll tell you what to feel
and think and do and say

we'll tell you when to smile
and we'll tell you when to cry
we'll tell you what is best for you
and try to tell you why

but what's best for the tiger
isn't what's best for the clown
and the tightrope walker's main concern
is falling to the ground

for some it's no big deal
and for some it's life and death
but we all are playing Ringmaster
and thinking we know best

and if you dare to disagree
and if you speak your mind
we'll attack behind our curtain
whilst on stage we roar #bekind

we'll tell you that you're wrong
although we'll never hear your point
for we're far too busy listening
to our own self-righteous voice

so welcome to our circus
where you're criticised for free
but whoops, did I say circus?
see I meant society

be grateful...

always

sunset

the sun wakes up each morning
and she combs her fiery hair
and she sometimes holds the clouds aloft
so we don't see her there

she settles to her work
a never-ending nine to five
and she ticks off all her jobs to do
like keeping Earth alive

she's busy every moment
working hard behind the scenes
but you tell her she does nothing
for you judge by what you've seen

you criticise the grey sky
and you curse the dampened day
you moan it's cold and dreary
and the sun's the one to blame

and it's only when she's setting,
when she's off to work elsewhere
that you all a sudden recognise
the colours in her hair

see the saddest thing of all
is that she's been here all the time
but you fail to see her beauty
'til she's fading from the sky

what is a pretty face without a beautiful soul?

the tower

you stand and face the mirror
and you magnify your flaws
you focus on the features
that are so uniquely yours

but their uniqueness doesn't matter
for they simply don't conform
to the criteria of beauty
they've convinced you is the norm

they make believe that beauty
doesn't go beneath your skin
that you simply can't be pretty
if you have a crooked grin

they say your eyes can't be too small
your nose can't be too big
that your lips must be just right
not over full and not too thin

they say your ears must not stick out
your hair can't be too wild
only those with tick-box beauty
may be physically admired

but those obsessed by beauty
are the ones who can't be free
because they're limited by what
somebody else says they should be

so next time you face the mirror
and you smile your crooked grin
remember beauty's just a tower
that society's trapped you in

and you think you can't escape
because you think there is no key
but you simply need to redefine
the walls of your beauty

are you showing
your true colours?

smoke and mirrors

mirror, mirror on the wall
is what she chose to paint
from colours green with envy,
red with anger, tinged with hate

she was aiming for reflection
when they gazed upon her art
but she had, without intention
shown them what was in her heart

see, it turns out what she'd painted
wasn't actually a mirror
but a door through which they saw
the things she'd tried to keep well hidden

for how she saw the world
and, with it, everybody else
was just an observation of
the way she saw herself

she painted insecurity,
regret and jealousy
and her brush dripped drops of bitterness
on every single piece

she thought she had attacked them
with her mirror on the wall
but she'd simply just revealed
what made her sad and vulnerable

so when you paint a picture
of the world you find out there
consider all the colours
that you wash upon the air

and consider if the picture
that you paint is actually true
and if it tells you about them
or tells them far more about you

imagine a nation

that prioritised

imagination

the jar

there was a little dreamer who,
from just the age of three,
spent all his time imagining
what he could do and be

he wanted to invent and
give the world something brand new
he wanted to change lives
even if he only changed a few

his wild imagination
was like a jar without a lid
and they nurtured and encouraged it
whilst he was still a kid

but as he grew and his dreams
showed no signs that they would slow
they tried to tame and rein them in
and screw the jar lid closed

they told him he should think
more realistically instead
yet almost everything that's real
was once thought up in someone's head

if everyone stopped dreaming
we'd be stuck right where we are
yet they tell us that, as adults,
we must live inside the jar

so, he parked his dreams up in the clouds,
said he'd return some day
but his dreams grew all redundant
as his life got in the way

yes, the dreamer stopped his dreaming
and they were all left wondering why
well, they said the sky's the limit
then put a ceiling on the sky

we are all

a river

the river

we look upon the map which shows
the river's winding course
we can see how it meanders
and can trace it to its source

we can see the little blue lines
representing every bend
and can follow them from where they start
until their journey's end

but though we see the river
with its curves and turns and twists
we must not assume we know it
for it's so much more than this

see, what a map can't show us
is how fast the water flows
how that water's warm in summer
how it freezes when it snows

it can't show how the water level
rises with the rain
or show all the plants and creatures
that the river can contain

it doesn't show the children
who have played along its banks
how it's turquoise blue in daytime
but at midnight shimmers black

a map can't show the families
who have picnicked at its edge
or the lovers who have kissed there
or the faces it reflects

see, we think we know the river
but it far exceeds our thoughts
for we're forgetting all the stories
that have thrived along its course

yes, we may see how it starts and ends
and turns and doubles back
but a river's so much more
than little blue lines on a map

so close...

almost

he almost took the bus that day
the number fifty-four
and she almost got off early
at the stop outside his door

he almost stopped for coffee
in the café where she served
and she almost cashed a cheque in
at the bank in which he worked

he almost walked straight into her,
engrossed so in his phone
when she almost crossed the path he
walked
but crossed over the road

he almost met a friend out
in a bar that Friday night
and she almost sang his favourite song
on the same bar's open mic

he almost queued behind her
at the midnight taxi rank
and she almost caught a glimpse of him
as he was walking past

he almost aced his interview
the following Monday
and she almost didn't take the job
'cos it was far away

but he didn't and she didn't
save for that one time she did
he was almost nearly hers
and she was almost nearly his

yes, they almost were an always
and they almost fell in love
but almost's as good as never
and almost was not enough

painting by numbers
is fun, but painting
without numbers
is freedom

outnumbered

7lbs 10oz
they all ask how much you weighed
and an IQ of 100
makes you average so they say

9 out of 10 in Monday's test
piano to grade 5
2 minors in your Friday test
and now you're free to drive

85's the pass mark
so you'd better try your best
and if you're scoring 90
then you're destined for success

but grade five doesn't tell them
of your favourite song to play
and how much you love is not defined
by how much you might weigh

seven pounds won't tell them
you were born to paint the stars
and your test scores can't explain
how you have come to bear your scars

two is not nostalgia
when you drive yourself back home
and it's not the memories you make
with friends out on the road

eighty-five and ninety
aren't the songs you sing when sad
and they're not the feeling in your heart
when you get up to dance

one hundred doesn't tell them
that your favourite month's September
so when you feel outnumbered
it's important you remember

you are strength and you are kindness,
you're creative and you're brave,
you are things that can't be measured,
can't be counted, can't be weighed

you're a name and not a number
you weren't born to be a score
so don't let them quantify you
when you're made of so much more

if our exterior was
all that mattered
then why would we
have all this wonder
in our souls?

inside story

they saw her in the library
discarded on a chair
and her glossy, shiny cover
made them notice she was there

they picked her up and held her
for a minute, maybe three
and they said she was exquisite
the most beautiful they'd seen

they thought not of her pages
simply stared at her in awe
then they put her on the bookshelf
as they headed out the door

so they never knew the words she chose
to mark her journey's start
and they didn't read the reams and reams
of kindness at her heart

they didn't read the things she hid
in pages left untouched
or the hellos and goodbyes she'd said
to people that she loved

they didn't read the chapters
where she set herself apart
and they never read the lines she wrote
of how they'd played their part

they didn't turn the pages
of her struggles and her strengths
and they missed the ripped-up paper
where she'd torn herself to shreds

they never read the parts
about the places she had been
or the people she had helped
and all the wonders she had seen

so when anybody asked them
what it was that she was like
they realised they had no idea
what she was like inside

see they'd told her she was beautiful
because of how she looked
but they'd just admired her cover
and they'd never read her book

Part Two

Lost

the pain is always
there – it's just
that life grows
around it

the rainbow door

her house was known to everyone
who lived for miles around
a talking point in homes and streets
and villages and towns

its shape and size were just the same
as others on the street
for it wasn't walls and windows
that had made her house unique

see she'd painted her front door
in every single rainbow hue
'til it stood in technicolour
yellows, purples, pinks and blues

and people came to see it
from a hundred different places
and they photographed her rainbow
with a smile upon their faces

but one day in September
on a windy, wet Monday
everybody turned their cameras
so they faced the other way

the street was full of photographs
of doors of red and green
with children stood outside of them
all uniformed and keen

and as she watched them leaving
for the school run in the rain
she leant against her front door
and she broke down from the pain

then she sat and cried a river
as she broke a little more
for the one she'd never photograph
outside that rainbow door

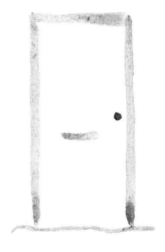

there's light in
there somewhere
I promise

the dark

he lives inside the forest
and there's few who enter in
for he lives right in the centre
where it's dangerous and dim

to reach him at his middle
there's a gauntlet you must run
through the trees and past the creatures
that stand guard against the sun

see he's used to feeling nothing,
used to sitting in the dark,
he feels safe under his canopy
that blocks out all the stars

but now and then a sliver
of pure sunlight filters through
and it's such a rare occurrence
that he's not sure what to do

it feels like it may burn him
with its piercing molten rays
and he has to shield his eyes
for fear it's setting him ablaze

its light is overwhelming
and he's choking on its warmth,
it's illuminating shadows
that he's trying to ignore

so he strengthens his defences
to drive out the sun's warm touch
for he'd rather feel nothing
than feel everything too much

he gathers up more branches
and he weaves in extra twigs
he makes sure his roof is light-proof
and the sun can't creep back in

and a sign outside the forest
warns you 'enter if you dare'
and if you're one who dares to enter
then you'd better be prepared

you're going to meet some monsters
and you'll stumble in the dirt
you'll be tempted to escape
to stop yourself from getting hurt

but if you reach the middle
sit and talk with him a while
and convince him life's for living
and not just to be survived

and tell him, though it's dark here,
that the reason he exists
is that the stubborn sun's still shining
and she won't give up on him

one of the biggest
lies in all the world
is "I'm fine"

sinking

there's thunder trapped inside her

there's a storm that lies within

there's a hurricane that's building

and it's growing with the wind

there's a tsunami behind her eyes

an ocean in her lungs

and she's navigating waters

she's not sure she'll overcome

for there's a ship she's sailing

that contains no maps or gold

just the hurricanes and thunder

that are trapped within her soul

and on her stormy ship

she finds it's easier to coast

than to drop her heavy anchor

and ask for help to stay afloat

she's struggling and lost at sea

and feeling all adrift

but because she's not capsized yet

they don't think she'll ever sink

but gradually the water

starts to creep over the edge

and the hurricanes and thunder

start to rear their angry heads

she panics as this perfect storm

starts swirling all around

and the ship fills ever faster

as the current pulls her down

then the ocean that consumes her

starts to fill her even more

'til her every breath is fighting

to avoid the ocean floor

and they never thought to question

when she said her ship was safe

so they slowly watch her sinking

'til they realise it's too late

it is quite possible
to be full of
emptiness

empty/full

he wasn't one to talk much
so instead of speaking up
he had silenced all the feelings
that were screaming from his gut

he'd bottled all his fury
stored his sadness in a jar
he had boxed up his anxiety
and covered all his scars

he put the jars and bottles
and the boxes on a shelf
and he carried on pretending
that containing them would help

but one day as he bottled
several jars of liquid doubt
he wondered would it help
if he had never let it out?

so he drank up his frustrations
his mistakes and his regrets
and he drained the bottles filled
with all the words he'd never said

he drank down all his anger
and he drank up all his pain
and they tasted like a poison
that was flooding through his brain

and as he sat surrounded
by the mess upon the floor
he knew he couldn't bottle up
his feelings anymore

for though the shelves lay empty
his thoughts filled him to the brim
and even though he'd drunk them
it was them consuming him

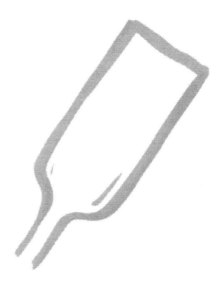

to be understood

is to be truly seen

the wolf and the willow

I'll tell you all a story
of an animal and tree
a wild and weeping willow
who was gentle as could be

and a wolf cub who was known
throughout the woods in which he lived
for the anger and aggression
and the hate that haunted him

see one night, when the moon was full
the wolf cub, all alone,
ran full speed through the forest
'til he reached the willow's home

he clawed and mauled her branches
and he growled an angry song
but she'd heard about this wolf cub
so she asked him what was wrong

and with narrowed eyes he bared his teeth
and then threw back his head
but the words he meant to howl
were not the words he actually said

his howling spoke of longing
of regret and jealousy
he told her "I am not enough
I hate that I am me"

he roared out in frustration
and his howls were loud with grief
and the noise grew even louder
as his crying brought relief

he told her he was terrified
that he was feeling trapped
and she realised howling at the moon
was his way to react

then the howling slowly faded
and his beating chest grew still
then he closed his mouth and looked down
and his eyes began to fill

"they say I can't belong here
that I'm just too full of hate
running angry and confused
towards a lost and lonely fate"

"you're not," the willow told him
"you don't have to be alone"
then she stood in peaceful silence
'til he realised he was home

and the willow's gentle branches
then embraced the young wolf cub
"you're not full of hate," she whispered
"you've just been so drained of love"

be the light

in someone's

dark

help

there's a knot inside her stomach
there are scratches on her arms
there's a weight upon her shoulders
that sits heavy on her heart

shadows lie beneath her eyes
where she can't get to sleep
and her breath is almost empty
and she trembles when she speaks

the shadows are like tissues
that are there to catch her tears
and the knot inside her stomach's
like a friend she's known for years

the heavy weight she carries
is like a blanket or a quilt
and the scars upon her body
are like battlements she's built

these things have all convinced her
they are there to keep her safe
to protect her from the dangers
and disasters she might face

and I know you want to help her
for her sadness breaks your heart
and, although it won't be easy,
there are simple ways to start

listen so she feels heard
and look to truly see
and don't hand her expectations
of who you think she should be

just be her friend and catch her tears
and wrap her up in love
and help her fight the voice inside
that says she's not enough

shhhhhh...

listen

listen when it's raining
as the water hits the ground
and you'll hear a million secrets
that are hidden in that sound

the pitter patter raindrops
hold the whispered words inside
of the people who have shared them
with the velvet midnight sky

the drops that pound the pavement
spill out anger loud and harsh
from the words and thoughts of people
who have cried beneath the stars

the rain that adds to oceans
and their vast capacious flow
is the grief of people holding on
for fear of letting go

the waters flooding cities
overwhelming homes and towns
are the silent words of suffering
entrusted to the clouds

and when the clouds are heavy,
when our secrets fill the sky,
when our thoughts are too oppressive
then the Earth begins to cry

so listen when it's raining
if you're quiet then you'll hear
all the secrets and emotions
that are muffled by Earth's tears

what is scarier -

being alone in a crowd

or alone with our own thoughts?

birdsong

she walked along the pathway
and she hadn't walked for long
when she met a little bird
who sang a melancholy song

she listened for a moment
to his sad, enchanting sound
and she asked him why he sang his song
when no-one was around

"I sing to tell the forest
that the day has just begun
and I join the morning chorus
as we're welcoming the sun

I sing so all the other birds
will know they're not alone
and I hum to all the trees
to help their leaves and branches grow

I sing for all the creatures
as they go about their day
and I whistle warnings to the sky
that clouds are on their way"

"but why," she asked him gently
"is your song so bittersweet?
why does it sound like longing
and like yearning when you tweet?"

"I sing to feel less lonely,"
said the tiny, little bird
"and I tweet into the quiet
just so I can feel heard

for when the sun is busy,
when the other birds have flown,
when the trees are climbing skyward
then I'm left here on my own

and I sing to ask the questions
that are tearing through my mind
but I don't know what I fear the most
silence... or the reply"

if you are secure in yourself, you will not fear making others your equal

the cage

they lock the tiger in the cage
it's how It's always been
and though she's fed and exercised
she's never actually free

the other tigers tell her
that it's just their lot in life
and that resignation's easier
than standing up to fight

but she's desperate for her freedom,
her autonomy and choice
so she claws the bars and growls at them
and prays they hear her voice

and though she's the one that's locked up
they think they're under attack
so they strike the cage and tell her
that she's just a little cat

but if she's "just a cat"
powerless as they've portrayed
then what are they so scared of?
what makes them so afraid?

see if their superiority's
so certain and secure
then why don't they simply take the key
and just unlock her door?

no... they know if they release her
then she might just show them all
the strength and fierce intelligence
and power in her roar

and of course, they do not want that
for then things might have to change
so they hide behind what's always been
and keep her in her cage

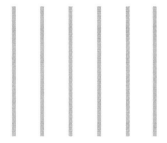

but can you really
handle the storm?

the rain

you said you loved the rain
and that you weren't scared of the dark
you said that you could carry
heavy things within your arms

you said you were not shallow
you saw beauty in the broken
you were comfortable in silence
left by thoughts and words unspoken

but when you held their heavy heart
you had to put it down
and when their tears washed over you
you thought that you might drown

their dark was far too dark for you
your eyes could not adjust
and you told them that their broken parts
made them too hard to love

it seems you loved their silence
just as long as you could speak
and you swam amongst their shallows
when their feelings ran too deep

you sheltered from their stormy skies
in spite of what you claimed
see, why put up your umbrella
if you say you love the rain?

this is not

the end

ouraboros

her wings were spun from sunsets
and from fading Autumn leaves,
from sycamore seed skeletons
and dandelion seeds

she wove in supernovas
with some scattered clouds sewn in,
they were delicate and fragile
barely-there and paper-thin

her wings of nearly-nothing
were at odds with all the rest
that were forged by flaming meteors
and blazed with fiery strength

but she didn't need such power
just a gentleness instead,
for she sought the ones who fought
a raging battle in their heads

she found them at their darkest,
in their all-consuming night,
so she spread out her translucent wings
and let in pools of light

she saw them in their slumber
whispering forgotten dreams,
so she plucked a wish from in her wings
and threw it to the breeze

she recognised their winter,
frozen cold and bleak with snow,
so she wrapped them in the embers
of her incandescent glow

and the rest thought she was broken
with her wings so nearly dead
but if they had watched her closely
they'd have seen that every thread

in her wings of seeds and sunsets
simply echoed loud her cause:
to convince the lost and desperate
everything can be reborn

Part Three

Found

do not become

the thing you

loathe

roar

as children we're convinced
that monsters hide beneath our beds
but as adults we soon realise
that they walk the streets instead

it's not their face that's monstrous
it's their loathing and their lies
for it's not about the way they look
it's who they are inside

they roar a song of malice,
manipulation, power, greed
and they feast upon our silence
thinking we admit defeat

and, at first, we tiptoe round them
terrified to make a noise
but slowly, very surely,
we are bound to find our voice

then, as fear gives way to anger
and as our loathing multiplies,
we start becoming monstrous
and we think we're justified

but flames won't put out fire,
water will not halt a flood
and we cannot stop the monsters
by behaving as they would

see anyone who's ever loved
somebody else before
knows no matter how much hate we feel
love always matters more

so though you're brave to fight them
and your courage makes you tough
don't fight them out of hate
but to protect the things you love

and when life gets too scary
promise me you'll make sure
that you won't become a monster
but you'll still learn how to roar

if your best argument
is the other side's weaknesses
what does that say about
your strengths?

the sand and the snow

one year, in late December
the desert met the snow
and she had to shield her eyes
against the glistening pure-white glow

the sight unnerved her greatly
as her breath caught on the air
for she'd never seen a girl like this
with snowflakes in her hair

she felt a little threatened
for how could they both exist?
how could there be the room on earth
for total opposites?

so she told Snow she was far too cold
and hard to walk upon
and that friends would lose their fingers
if they sat with her too long

but Snow said not to worry
for her friends all came prepared
see she made sure they all knew
the gloves and coats and boots to wear

yet Sand said they'd still perish
in the blizzards and the storms
for amidst the freezing temperatures
no coat could keep them warm

so Snow showed her a shelter
that was freezing-cold to touch
but inside it gave protection
when the weather got too much

Sand argued it was bleak here
and so stark and ugly too
she could scarcely feel the sunshine
in the sky of icy blue

then Snow walked up the mountain
with Sand following behind
and she radiated beauty
as the sun began to rise

and Sand just kept on talking
'til there were no more words to say
until all her criticisms
had been melted clean away

see Snow had rightly proved herself
and proud and tall she'd stand
for she'd done it without saying
a single word against the sand

do not be afraid

of your tears

the dam

she'd built herself a dam
so she could hold her tears at bay
a wall of stubborn barricade
to keep her pain away

her barriers were busyness
distraction and denial
and ignoring and avoiding's
how she coped for quite a while

but the trouble was, her dam left
nowhere for her pain to go
so it sat behind her wall
with nothing left to do but grow

the tightening in her chest
began constricting every breath
and to battle every painful thought
took every ounce of strength

the lump inside her throat
got slightly bigger every day
and before too long she found
she couldn't blink her tears away

so the pressure kept on building
and the dam began to crack
and it soon became impossible
to hold the water back

so she let the dam burst open
and as she felt the water flow
she realised sometimes all we need
is just to let it go

butterfly kisses

are my favourite

– so gentle and

intimate

the butterfly

"trade me a memory," the butterfly said
"a memory that's heavy and harsh
and I'll sit and I'll listen and try my sweet best
to lighten the load on your heart"

so he told her of struggles, of heartache and pain
and he cried as he spoke them aloud
for it wasn't one memory but lots of the same
that were, all of them, weighing him down

he spoke of a place filled with darkness and fear,
a tunnel devoid of all hope
then the spots on her wings deftly captured his tears
and softly and gently she spoke

"thanks for the memories," she said with a smile
then she gave him a butterfly kiss
then she drew a deep breath as she wistfully sighed
and then traded her memory for his

"I've always been me, but not always like this
there was once when I thought I had died
I was shrouded in darkness 'til I grew my wings
see, I needed that darkness to fly

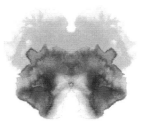

people will never

forget how you

treated them

the fall

he clambers up his ladder
made from them and him and her
and he tramples on their faces
like he's trampling through some dirt

then he sits atop his tower
and ignores their cries for help
for he now no longer needs them
and he's happy by himself

he sits consumed by ego,
by his hierarchy and power
whilst his ladder help each other
to ascend a different tower

but one day comes a dragon
breathing flames of fiery green
and the man atop the tower
knows that he must quickly leave

so he calls out to his ladder
but they all decline the call
and as his tower slowly crumbles
they sit back and watch him fall

never forgotten

always loved

wave of light

the others lit their candles
for the ones who couldn't be
for the memories of the angels
who would now forever sleep

she tried to light the matches
but they snapped within her hand
and he took her hands in his
to show that he could understand

they sat there for a moment
as the candle sat in wait
then he struck a match and lit it
and they gazed upon the flame

but the light that flickered brightly
almost burned their eyes at once
and the flames that licked against their
skin
were hurting far too much

and the shadows from the candle
brought an overwhelm of pain
for the heartbeats and the movements
and the pictures blurry grey

so they breathed the heat and fire in
then blew it out to smoke
and as the candle settled then
they held each other close

and whilst others lit their candles
they chose not to take their part
but it didn't dim the flame of love
that burned within their hearts

some things can be

light as a feather in your

arms but heavy in your heart

baggage

she opens up her suitcase
and it's loaded to the brim
she simply doesn't have the room
to squeeze more baggage in

that holdall's filled with years and years
of things she has endured
but you think she has no holdall
for she acts all self-assured

but just because she's confident
and acts like she's alright
it doesn't mean her baggage
is inconsequentially light

'cos though her life looks rosy
it doesn't mean to say
that she doesn't carry burdens
that will weigh her down each day

she's fought off many monsters
often swam up from the depths
she's walked through many fires
and pulled herself back from the edge

so never think she walks on air
when she's actually walked through hell
you just don't know her load is heavy
'cos she carries it so well

silence has a
lot to answer for

silence

it was the Sunday market
and, as I wandered down the aisles,
an older woman weaving
made me stop and watch a while

she wove a little blanket
but the thread she used was odd
for it wasn't wool or yarn she used
but words pulled from a pot

she threaded up her needle
with a string of "I love you"
and she wove them into "help me"
braided with "I miss you too"

then "no" a hundred times
rose from her pot as silver thread
and I saw that she had named her stall
'blankets of regret'

and, as I stood and watched her then,
I saw 'I love you' fade
and 'help me' slowly disappeared
and 'no' began to wane

her words had now become a quilt
of pale translucency
and I asked if I could hold this thing
that I could barely see

I expected light and air
but it lay heavy in my hands
and I had to ask about it
for I had to understand

so I asked, "what are you weaving?"
and she told me, "everyday
I weave the silence left by words
we're too afraid to say"

be the lifeboat

in somebody's

storm

the storm

she'd been aboard her boat now
in a storm that raged for weeks
when she caught sight of two people
who were lost and all at sea

one looked all exhausted
as he swam against the tide
and the other gasped for every breath
just trying to survive

she looked on in confusion
for they must have had a boat
so now why were they without it?
and she called out to them both

"you should have kept yourselves aboard
and not abandoned ship
you should have worn a life jacket
and better learnt to swim"

and in between their fight for life
they tried hard to explain
that their boat had been destroyed
by bolts of lightning, wind and rain

but she barely heard their reason
for, whilst she sat safe and dry,
she'd failed to see how hard they'd worked
to keep themselves alive

then as she watched them suddenly
engulfed by violent waves,
her fortune and her privilege
engulfed her just the same

she realised quite uncomfortably
that she was still afloat
only since she had been lucky
to avoid a damaged boat

so, instead of blaming, shouting at them
telling them to swim,
she threw them both a lifeline
and she pulled them safely in

then not much later afterward
the sky became less grey
and the waves grew ever calmer
and they heard the thunder fade

and she realised, as they sat there
and they watched the storm die down,
that it felt far better helping
than if she had watched them drown

heart

earth

mother earth

she's mountains and she's sunshine
she's the moon, silvery bright
she's the clouds and wind and rain
and she's the dancing Northern Lights

she is deserts and savannahs
she's the waves that fill the sea
she is birdsong and she's flowers
she's the blossom on the trees

and if you treat her fairly
she will let the sun shine through
she will kiss you with a gentle breeze
and paint the sky in blue

she'll rain if you are thirsty
then she'll blow the clouds away
and she'll decorate with rainbows
whilst she calms the ocean waves

but if you treat her badly
she will breathe out stormy skies
she will summon up tornadoes
and antagonise the tides

she'll throw things from the mountain
in an avalanche of snow
and she'll blaze and burn the forest
so the trees no longer grow

she'll treat you as you treat her
so be careful what you choose
for she's power you can't comprehend
and much she stands to lose

so treat her with the kindness
and respect that she deserves
see, if you rearrange her heart
you'll see it holds the earth

the world is always

darker at night

4am

I met with 4am last night
she said to say hello
and she said she's seen a lot of you
since several weeks ago

she said she hears your worries
when you're lying there awake
but she'd rather watch you sleeping
with a smile upon your face

so she's gathered up your worries
and she feeds them to the stars
and they swallow them with fire
'til they're left with only half

then they whisper to the sun
as she begins her morning climb
and the sunshine takes your worries
and accepts them every time

she chops them into pieces
'til she's left with merely grains
then she throws them to the clouds
so they can gently fall as rain

and the sunlight then transforms
your drops of worry into hope
so that rainbow that you see?
that's 4am saying hello

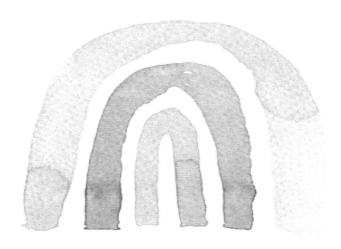

hope is every

colour under

the sun

hope

he stood and faced his canvas
and he opened up his tin
but the tin lay bare and empty
for it had no colours in

his paintbrush hovered ready
but he had nothing to paint
for the world felt tired and weary
and the skies were dark and grey

but then, a little robin
chose his palm on which to land
and his paintbrush stroked its red chest
as it rested on his hand

then he found a tiny fire
and his paintbrush stirred the flames
for the sparks of dancing orange
were the perfect fiery shade

he looked up at the sun
and felt its warmth against his skin
whilst drops of molten yellow
starting pooling in his tin

he walked into the forest
and once there he found a tree
and his paintbrush took green samples
from its many different leaves

he lasso-ed all the clouds
to leave a sky of flawless blue
then swirled his paintbrush through the air
collecting all its hues

he sailed out to the ocean
where it's wide and vast and deep
and his brush created ripples
in the indigo-blue sea

he headed to his garden
where the world was calm and quiet
and he found the perfect purple
on the petals of a violet

he put what he'd collected
all together in a pot
and he mixed 'til he was happy
with the colours that he got

then instead of to his canvas
to the air his paintbrush went
painting ribbons of bright colours
mixed from tones that nature sent

and his colours waved their banners
with their message soaring high
for he'd painted hope with rainbows
and he'd draped them 'cross the sky

growing

through it

growth

there's a tree that I've been watching
and I see it in my dreams
for it calls to me and whispers
as its leaves blow in the breeze

and though the roots are hidden
and now shrouded from the light
I know for sure without them
I'd have never climbed so high

it whispers of a struggle
from the roots up through the trunk
and from there it tells of healing
grown from nurture, care and love

so now when I am doubtful
and become unsure of me
I'll close my eyes and listen
to the whispers of that tree

and here emerge the many branches
stretching far and wide
growing, blooming, blossoming
and reaching for the sky

and as these blossoms open up
encouraged by the sun
I take a step back from the tree
and see it all as one

I see it tells a story
of a journey over time
and I realise it's my story
and the journey all is mine

I've reached the upper branches
but the trunk stands strong below
for it's all the love and healing
that's enabled me to grow

you'll find that, sooner or
later, there are bridges
you no longer need to cross

burning bridges

she stood upon her bridge
and watched the water flow beneath
and a voice inside her head explained
that life was like this stream

it told her certain things in life
are never meant to last
that their destiny's to flow towards
the ocean of our past

it said that clinging on to these
would tire and exhaust her
that the current meant she'd fight
a losing battle with the water

but then she told the voice of times
the stream had quenched her thirst
or had cooled her in the summer heat
and carried things to her

the voice said, yes, that there were times
the stream had cooled and quenched
but there were also times it flooded her
and left her drowned and drenched

she knew the voice was right
and that she had to let it go
that she'd spent so long upon her bridge
watching the stream below

so the voice produced a box
and clean against it struck a match
and she watched it spark to life
and saw the tiny fire dance

and as the dance grew brighter then
she tossed it to the ground
and, as she bid a bittersweet farewell,
she watched her bridge burn down

a heart full

of fire

fine

"do not go near the flames," he said
"beware the sparks and heat
be careful of the white-hot ash
that burns beneath your feet"

"fret not," she said, "come closer
as these flames grow ever higher
and you'll see I have nothing to fear
for I'm the whole damn fire"

Part Four

Return to You

books can take us

anywhere in the universe

in fact, they can take us

to places that don't even exist

- that is true magic

a new chapter

she asked him how he'd done it
how he'd built marshmallow towns
how he'd met a little poor boy
who was destined for the crown

she asked him how he knew
about the language fairies speak
and how he'd caught a shooting star
that now was his to keep

she asked him how he'd touched the clouds
without a pair of wings
and how he'd heard the music
of a chestnut tree that sings

she asked him how he'd swum
right to the bottom of the sea
and how he'd watched a mountain cry
and heard the sunshine speak

she found it all a mystery -
she breathed the air he breathed
but he breathed out tales of distant lands
and things she'd never seen

and she saw a world of wonder
when she looked up close at him
and when he spoke, his words flowed
like a poem on the wind

he told her that it hadn't been
some wings that helped him fly
and it hadn't been a net he'd used
to catch things from the sky

it wasn't maps that led him
to a chest of buried gold
and it hadn't been a ship that sailed him
halfway round the world

it wasn't bricks he'd used
to build a castle in the sky
for he told her he had lived
all of these wonders in his mind

and he told her she could do it too
for reading's all it took
and she'd open up her world
if she just opened up a book

if they doubt you

do it anyway

suntrap

they told her she was crazy
for trying to catch the sun
and they said it was impossible
and never had been done

they said she'd burn her fingers
that it all would be waste
that the sun would soon consume her
in its searing, golden flames

but they never actually realised
that she moved on their behalf
for the world was getting colder
and the days were growing dark

so she did what was impossible
she did what no-one had
and she didn't char or smoulder
or reduce herself to ash

she gently caught the sun
without a struggle or a fight
so the world got slowly warmer
and the days were filled with light

then they crowded all around her
as their faith within her grew
for she'd done without exception
what they said she'd never do

they found her most enchanting
and, as she radiated awe,
they used her light to find themselves
and basked within her warmth

and they wondered how she'd done
and escaped without a burn
well, it turns out she was fire
and the sun belonged to her

an ocean of

love

I am your harbour

I am your harbour
and you are my sea
for I am your safe place
and you are my free

teaching me love
I had not known before
with still many depths
that I'm yet to explore

your waves and their power
all fill me with wonder
and keep me afloat
when I think I'll go under

some days you'll break
and you'll billow and crash
and some days you'll ripple
a soft, gentle splash

you're a constantly moving
continuous flow
and when it's relentless
I want you to know

whenever your tide
has grown tired of its ebb
sail back to the harbour
and there you can rest

for I am your harbour
and you are my sea
I am part of you
and you are part of me

and there's layers and depths
that I never had known
until I had two oceans
all of my own

the stars wrote
our story a long
time ago

serendipity

one night a star exploded
and it split right in to two
and each part became a person
one was me and one was you

we shimmered down to Earth
and lived our individual lives
but one day serendipity
decided we'd collide

your face felt so familiar
and every time you spoke
it sounded like a harmony,
a song I'd always known

it was like you were an ocean
that I wanted to explore
but the waves I surfed, the depths I swam
I felt I'd swum before

it felt like I knew nothing
and yet everything as well
as if me getting to know you
helped me get to know myself

I think the universe intended
and had planned this all along
to return me to your ocean
to your face and to your song

see it's not that you completed me
for I was never half
but it seems the stardust in our souls
could not be kept apart

memories are
like little portals
to the past

back in time

he walked across the field
when he came upon a stile
and he almost turned around
'cos he'd already walked for miles

but then he heard a melody
that made him carry on
it was a faint and distant echo
of an old familiar song

he walked towards the music
and it led him past a sign
to a row of houses starting
at the number ninety-nine

and from that house the scent
of childhood dinners filled the air
and he smelt the heady perfume
that his grandma used to wear

the next house on the path
was somehow number thirty-four
and it had a stained-glass window
of a rose within the door

he peered in through the window
of the next house down the street
and he saw familiar photographs
upon the mantlepiece

he heard some children laughing
so he looked over a fence,
where he saw a young boy playing
in the garden with his friends

they were splashing in a paddling pool
and playing with a ball
they were practising their cartwheels
and their handstands at the wall

and something like nostalgia
made him stand there for a while
'til he tore himself away and turned
and headed for the stile

and it was then he passed the signpost
with an all-familiar name
and he realised he had just walked down
a street called Memory Lane

sooner or later

the sun will shine

the flowers will bloom

and spring will come

spring

they met her on the corner
and she said her name was Spring
and she told them she'd been resting
whilst the winter did its thing

she'd watched behind the window
as the rain had turned to snow
and she'd lit herself a fire
when the wind began to blow

she'd watched the winter ravage
and strip bare the stubborn trees
whilst she'd sewn and stitched together
brand new blossoms and their leaves

she said when it was cold
that she'd been sleeping in the warm
and when winter brought its blizzards
she'd been singing through the storm

when frosty mornings lingered
she'd been busy planting seeds
and, until she could pick flowers,
she had picked a book to read

and she told them, through the bleakness
she'd been writing to the sun
and the sun wrote back 'hang in there,
there are brighter days to come'

then they looked at her and realised
there were flowers in her hair
and her smile was bright and sunny
and her voice had warmed the air

then she waved and she was gone
but in her wake, she left them hope
and they knew the sun was on its way
to gently thaw the snow

and they felt a sense of peace
about what future days might bring
when they realised every winter
must be followed by the spring

what will you leave behind?

the storyteller

the pub I was in
smelt of wine and cigars
when I saw two old men
who were sat by the bar

then I looked at the group
where the other man spoke
and they laughed 'til they cried
as he told them a joke

one was surrounded
by laughter and cheers
the other was sitting
alone with his beers

so I took myself over
and stood at the back
and noticed he hadn't got
cases or sacks

I felt really bad
for the man on his own
so I walked up and pulled up
a stool of my own

but the stories he told
of the oceans he'd sailed
the countries he'd seen
and the mountains he'd scaled

and that's when I noticed
the stuff on the floor
the holdalls and trunks
and suitcases galore

his stories were epic
his life had been full
then he tapped on his glass
and he said to us all

"what's in them?" I asked
and he shrugged with a sigh
"just things I thought mattered,
the things I could buy."

"it's time I must go
but I've loved growing old
and I know I'll live on
through the tales that I've told

then he drank up his drink
and whilst shedding a tear
he smiled at me sadly
and then disappeared

please believe when I say
that to live is enough
your life should be measured
by memories not stuff."

and nobody noticed
'cos all he had left
was the stuff in the boxes,
the trunks and the chests

then he rose from his chair
and we all shed a tear
as he held up his drink to us
then disappeared

wrap yourself in

this busy

blanket of life

patchwork

your life is like a quilt
and everybody weaves their share
some weave huge great tapestries
whilst some weave tiny squares

there are squares that bring you laughter
and some that bring you tears
and some are stitched and sewn by those
who are no longer here

in places there are threads
of people choosing not to stay
and sometimes when you touch these threads
it brings back all the pain

but all the parts that hurt you
have slowly taught you how
to weave your contribution
into the blanket you have now

for every tiny thread
that tells of joy and pain and fun
has stitched a quilt together
of the person you've become

so I know there's squares that comfort you
and squares that you dislike
but without them all you wouldn't have
this patchwork of your life

you are capable
of more than you
ever thought possible

ripples

never let them tell you

that you cannot make a change

when the ripples of a single stone

can make a million waves

sometimes we have
to get lost to find
ourselves again

breathe

she sat at the back
and they said she was shy
she led from the front
and they hated her pride

they asked her advice
and then questioned her guidance
they branded her loud
then were shocked by her silence

when she shared no ambition
they said it was sad
so she told them her dreams
and they said she was mad

they told her they'd listen
then covered their ears
and gave her a hug
whilst they laughed at her fears

and she listened to all of it
thinking she should
be the girl they told her to be
best as she could

but one day she asked
what was best for herself
instead of trying
to please everyone else

so she walked to the forest
and stood with the trees
she heard the wind whisper
and dance with the leaves

and she spoke to the willow
the elm and the pine
and she told them what
she'd been told time after time

she told them she never
felt nearly enough
she was either too little
or far, far too much

too loud or too quiet
too fierce or too weak
too wise or too foolish
too bold or too meek

then she found a small clearing
surrounded by firs
and she stopped and she heard
what the trees said to her

and she sat there for hours
not wanting to leave
for the forest said nothing...
it just let her breathe

life is worth it

my darling

thirteen

dear thirteen, I hope you get this
and I hope it finds you well
see, I'm writing you this letter
for I have so much to tell

it's words – I hope – of wisdom
of insight and advice
some lessons that I pray
will help you navigate through life

the first is – life gets easier
and then gets hard again
but persevere because I know
it works out in the end

you're going to lose some people
and it's natural that you'll grieve
but you're going to make your peace
with those who choose to up and leave

there'll be times when you're in love
and they're not meant to last forever
but don't worry for the future's
saving someone even better

try your best at school
but do not give up on you dreams
it's never too late to be
what you've always wanted to be

you're going to hurt some people
you don't get to say you've not
but you get to say you're sorry
and you get to right your wrongs

there'll be times when others hurt you
when you're lied to and betrayed
but I promise you'll get stronger
and the hurt will slowly fade

so many things will happen
that will test your strength of mind
but you'll learn through all of it
that it takes nothing to be kind

and there's someone more important
than most everybody else
who deserves your love and kindness
and that person is... yourself

see, your life will all make so much sense
as soon as you can learn
to forgive and to embrace yourself
and recognise your worth

and how is it I know all this
of life and loss and love?
well, I've lived your years and many more
I'm you – just all grown up

is this not

the end?

the end?

when things come to a close

we sometimes ache for what we're missing

but what if every end

is actually just the next beginning...

If you need someone to talk to...

I know that some of the poems in this book can trigger some painful and difficult memories and emotions. I hope that, even if this is the case, you can find some peace, some support, or some comfort in the words.

But if it is all feeling too much then please don't struggle alone. You can always email me at talkingtothewild@outlook.com or direct message me on my social media channels:

Facebook – Talking to the Wild

Instagram - @talkingtothewild

TikTok - @talkingtothewild

You can also find support at the following websites:

www.hftd.org

www.rainbowtrust.org.uk

www.mind.org.uk

www.mentalhealth.org.uk

www.bliss.org.uk

www.live-evermore.org

www.nationalshare.org

www.mentalhealth.gov

www.differentbrains.org

Acknowledgements

I'd say that I don't know where to start but that's not strictly true. I'm just not sure where to finish. There are so, SO many people that I need to acknowledge for supporting me, believing in me, grounding me and inspiring me that I'm worried I'll run out of pages.

But I know exactly where to start: John. Thank you for always being my biggest cheerleader and for believing in me more than I often believe in myself. I could not and would not have written this book without you. I wouldn't have shared my poetry on social media, and I certainly wouldn't have had so many lovely notebooks and journals to write in! To be known, seen and loved so entirely is extraordinary. I love you.

To my boys – Rory and Archie. Thank you for inspiring me beyond measure. You are my greatest achievement and have taught me more about accepting myself than anything else ever has done. I love you in a way that even a poem about a harbour can't put into words.

To Mum and Dad – thank you doesn't quite cut it! You have always taught me that I can be and do anything I want and have supported me no matter what that 'anything' was. You raised me to be (I hope!) soft but strong, proud but gracious, kind but fair. So much of who I am is because of you both and because of the experiences and love you gave me growing up. Thank you.

To Clare, Phousa and Suki – you are what happens when love perseveres and endures. And because of that, you will always inspire me. Thank you.

To Nana – I wrote a book Nana! When I wrote 'Back in Time', I thought so much about toasting crumpets on the fire and Grampy's gold shorts and the time we April fooled you by telling you there was a lamb on the road! Thank you for

understanding the power of words and for encouraging such
a love of reading for me and now for our boys.

To all my friends who have been there through everything:
school lessons, life lessons, boyfriends, breakups, holidays,
heartbreak, good times, grief and all things in-between.
Thank you for loving me through every stage of my life –
even when I was difficult to love. You've been my confidantes,
my rocks, my inspiration, my work support, my cappuccino
buddy, my Shrek friend, my therapy, my dancing divas,
my uni girls, my escape room buddies, the bridesmaid to my
bride, the bride to my bridesmaid, my childhood memories,
my laughter lines, my happy minutes, my nights out, my
housemates, my ladies in red (minus the sleeves!), my filthy
gorgeous lady in purple and my karaoke queens. Thank you
for everything.

To my in-laws – Jackie, John, Sam and the boys. Thank you
for loving me as part of your family and for everything you
do for us all. I am so so thankful for all your support.

And last, but certainly not least, to everyone on social media
who doesn't know me personally but who has liked and shared
my poetry. You will never truly know how much your incredible
support and wonderful words of encouragement have meant to
me. You have inspired me so much without even realising it.
Even if all of this only lasts for a short while, you have changed
my life. Thank you.

Becky xxx

0c897f5c-2a44-473e-96cf-974d7959c49aR01